Dedication

To Joanne
for her love, patience,
and support of this book

CUSTOMER EXPERIENCE Rules!

52 ways to create a great customer experience

by JEOFREY BEAN

illustrated by STEVE HICKNER

BRIGANTINE MEDIA

Brigantine Media
211 North Avenue, St. Johnsbury, Vermont 05819
Phone: 802-751-8802 | Fax: 802-751-8804
Email: neil@brigantinemedia.com
Website: www.brigantinemedia.com

ISBN: 978-1-9384064-9-2

CUSTOMER EXPERIENCE Rules!

Acknowledgments

This book has been made possible with the support and encouragement from my family, friends, and colleagues—and by the many readers of the earlier book, *The Customer Experience Revolution*, who have asked me about the next book. I appreciate your passion and excellent ideas you shared with me about what the next book should be. You will see many of your suggestions on the following pages.

A very special thank you to my publisher Brigantine Media, Neil Raphel and Janis Raye. I appreciate your great ideas, creative energy, and publishing expertise. One of those great and creative ideas was having a business book illustrated by Steve Hickner!

To Steve Hickner, thank you for your fantastic illustrations! They engage and entertain, while emphasizing the essential points and emotions of each rule.

The heart and soul of *Customer Experience Rules!* is made of exceptional individuals who shared their time, expertise, and invaluable insights. They are:

- Ron Ahlensdorf Jr., President of Summit Valuations

- Sharon Carmichael, Senior Interaction Design Manager at Intuit

- Joely Gardner, PhD, CEO of Human

Factors Research

- Harry Hersh, Co-author of *The Human Factor: Designing Computer Systems for People*

- Steve Hickner, Illustrator of *Customer Experience Rules!* and Director and Producer at DreamWorks Animation

- Donald Norman, author of *Emotional Design: Why We Love (or Hate) Everyday Things* and Director, Design Lab at University of California, San Diego

- Tom Parham, Principal of Technology Leadership Services

- Janice Sutton, CEO and Executive Editor of *Fleet Management Weekly*

- Gary Tucker, CEO of DealerRater

- Sean Van Tyne, Co-author of *The Customer Experience Revolution* and Design Leadership Advisor - PlayStation™ Network - Sony Network Entertainment Int'l

The Rules

The Rules

Learn from the best.

GREAT CUSTOMER EXPERIENCE, when purposefully made and genuine, creates businesses that are better for customers, are more profitable, and last longer than others.

This kind of customer experience is engaging, and customers want to have it again and again. It creates advocates who share their experience on social media because they want others to experience it, too.

Like my first book, *The Customer Experience Revolution* (co-authored with Sean Van Tyne), *Customer Experience Rules!* is based on expertise combined with the latest research and in-person interviews of customer experience leaders. These leaders are passionate about determining, developing, and delivering extraordinary customer experiences.

Customer Experience Rules! focuses on 52 best practices common to the CX leaders who consistently improve or innovate their CX. I nickname these companies and their leaders "Experience Makers."

The Experience Makers mentioned in the book are at varying stages of company development. Some are in retail, business-to-business, or both. They include Uber, Tesla, Amazon, Qualcomm, Kaiser Permanente, DealerRater, Imprivata, Apple, Starwood Hotels, and more.

These 52 CX rules comprise a proven set of insights from Experience Makers that you can use to improve your company's customer experience. They show that, more than ever, customer experience has become a game-changer in many industries. CX has become the decisive measure of success.

That's why the first rule is: Be a customer experience leader (or bite the dust)!

Be a customer experience leader (or bite the dust).

COMPANIES WITH SUCCESSFUL customer experience are growing fast, pleasing customers, and leaving the competition in the dust. Companies without successful customer experiences are dying.

Customer Experience (CX) includes all the interactions people have *with* or *about* a company's messages, people, processes, products, and services. CX concerns the *totality* of the customer's interaction with a company.

Think branding. Add customer service. Stir in some social media. Spice with some advertising. Deliver a user experience that exceeds expectations. And voila! You've created a great customer experience for your customers.

Once you become a customer experience leader, you'll never turn back. When the customer is the center of the universe, you win—and your customers win.

Engage your CEO in customer experience.

CUSTOMER EXPERIENCE DOESN'T work its way up the organization. Commitment from the CEO is vital to instill a customer experience culture in a company.

Amazon's CEO Jeff Bezos says: "Our goal is to be earth's most customer-centric company."

Starbucks' CEO Howard Schultz says his company should be focused on customer experience. He wants Starbucks to be a place for conversation and community—a third place between work and home.

These leaders have made sure their company cultures embody their commitment to customers. If your leader is not committed to instilling world-class customer experience, your company will not rise to the top.

Know your "Do-Fors."

"DO-FORS" ARE WHAT your products or services actually *do for* customers. They are the heart of your advertising and answer these customer questions:

- "What will this product or service do for me?"

- "Why should I care about this product or service?"

- "Why should I invest my time or money in this product or service?"

These Do-Fors effectively communicate each company's value proposition:

Intuit SnapTax—"Snap It. Tap It. Done. Taxes

Done Right."

My Starbucks Rewards—"A loyalty program that's all about you – Get exclusive offers by simply registering a Starbucks Card."

Square (mobile device credit card solution)— "Start selling today. Clear pricing. Customer support. Serious security."

Qualcomm® Gobi™ 4G LTE technology— "Wireless freedom. Global network coverage."

Do-Fors: Ask not what your customers can do for you, but what you can Do-For your customers.

Release a product only when you are satisfied it's the best it can be.

DON'T ENTER THE market until you are ready to give customers an extraordinary experience. **Don't do it.**

Years ago at Apple, Steve Jobs went through more than a dozen versions of the Macintosh computer before he was satisfied that it was the best possible product for consumers. I learned about Jobs's philosophy of product introduction from Larry Tesler, former Vice President and Chief Scientist at Apple. According to Tesler, "Whether it was positioning the marketing message, or customer service and support, or upgrades and repairs, Steve Jobs usually said, 'delay

the product so you can fix it.'"

It is not enough to meet your internal production milestones if your customer experience will disappoint. Only launch when your message, products, and services are ready to give a great customer experience. That's what people will remember.

RULE
5

Steal the best customer experience practices from other industries.

YOUR CUSTOMERS ARE having experiences with every other company they do business with. All those experiences can impact their expectations for your company. But the best of those companies are probably not in your industry.

Here's an example. Your company sells outdoor gear. So you naturally assume your customer experience is compared to companies such as Cabela's, L.L. Bean, and REI. And it probably is. But it's just as likely that your customers also want your customer

CUSTOMER EXPERIENCE RULES!

experience to be like Nordstrom in its customer service, like Zingerman's in its knowledgable staff, and like National Car Rental in its speed of processing.

Your customers are more involved and informed than ever. You can't rely on merely being better than your direct competitors. The best customer experience businesses are influencing your customer, so you'd better be at the top of your game if you want to compete.

Find, capture, and keep customers with social media.

RUNNING A SUCCESSFUL business depends on finding, capturing, and keeping customers.

You've found your *active* customers. Active customers interact directly *with* your company's messages, people, process, products, and services.

You need to find, capture, and keep *potential* customers. Potential customers have indirect interactions *about* your company's messages, people, process, products, and services.

What people learn *about* your company is just as important as the experiences they have *with* it.

Today, social media is the gateway to new customers. LinkedIn, Facebook, Google Plus, YouTube,

Twitter, Instagram, Pinterest, and other social media open up new lines of communication about your company.

In 2014, Nielsen reported that 47 percent of smartphone owners visit social networks every day. Social media has revolutionized people's shopping experience anytime and anywhere there is Internet.

Be customer smart by being social media savvy.

High tech can trump high touch.

AMAZON'S CUSTOMER EXPERIENCE is ranked number one in Forrester's 2014 Customer Experience Index. Yet the vast majority of people dealing with Amazon never talk to a human! At Amazon, giving customers the information they need and the value they want in a timely fashion trumps human handholding.

In the brick-and-mortar world, solutions that help people perform routine transactions without human intervention can achieve high loyalty and customer advocacy rates. Think bank ATMs and airline check-in online and at kiosks.

The best customer experience doesn't necessarily mean dealing with a person at all, if the experience can be given more effectively through automation, algorithms, or even animatronics. Who wants to wait for a ride at Disney? No one. But high tech keeps customers entertained, even in long lines.

Watch out: Google is working on a high-tech customer experience to make driving without a human the ultimate road trip.

RULE
8

Study how your customers want to buy.

THE MORE YOU find out about your customers' buying habits, the better experience you can give them. If you're selling cars, you need to know the hotels your customers stay at, the computers they use, the supermarkets they shop.

Tesla's management believed that people who would buy a high-end, all-electric performance car had an aversion to the traditional car buying experience. They found that many of their potential customers were regular buyers of higher-end Apple products. These customers not only enjoyed the buyer experience in the Apple stores, they were advocates of it, and used it as their high bar for comparing all other in-store customer experiences.

So, in a move contrary to the internal promotion policies of most car companies, Tesla hired George Blankenship, who honed Apple's retail store customer experience. Blankenship made Tesla's dealerships operate like Apple stores. They provide consumers with friendly interactions in an open, no-pressure environment.

From 2010 through 2013, 25,000 Tesla Model S cars were sold—20 percent above the sales target.

It pays to know how your customers like to buy. And what they like about it.

Make your company name a verb.

TODAY, WE'RE GOOGLING to search online, Skyping to make a face-to-face phone call, and Ubering to ride from place to place. When customers use the company's name to describe the service, that's a great indication that they are happy with their customer experience.

Years ago, according to Nick Bilton in the *New York Times*, companies were concerned about losing their trademark status.

No more. Word-of-mouth and social media can accelerate the awareness of a start-up from one person to many in seconds. If this happens while a company is starting up, people may start associating the company name with the service.

So be a verb. Recognition is the sincerest form of flattery. Consider Tweeting about this book!

Give your customers a K.I.S.S.

FROM POLITICS TO technology, from selling to service, follow the K.I.S.S. rule (Keep It Simple, Stupid).

A corollary to this rule was developed by Steve Krug in his wonderful book, *Don't Make Me Think: A Common Sense Approach to Web Usability*. Krug says, "When I look at a web page it should be self-evident. Obvious. Self-explanatory. I should be able to 'get it'—what it is and how to use it—without expending any effort thinking about it."

It takes a lot of work to make a website simple and straightforward. When a customer comes to your website, he/she should immediately know how to use it. You have to determine what your customers want and need to know, and then create the best website to help them find that information.

For many companies, the website experience is the key customer interaction. Your website shouldn't make the customer think—just give them a K.I.S.S.!

Create two-pizza teams.

MANY COMPANIES ON the leading edge of creativity limit the size of their development teams for new products and services to a very small group. In fact, Jeff Bezos's rule to eradicate groupthink was to limit creative teams to about six people—a group that can be fed with two pizzas.

Intuit adopted the two-pizza team, too, when creating SnapTax. The small groups developed a big concept: "Finish your taxes in a snap. Grab your phone, snap a photo of your W-2 and get your taxes done right in as few as 10 minutes."

Make sure your new product and service development is not hampered by too many bodies and too many pizzas. Keep your creative staffing lean—and don't spare the pepperoni!

Invest in big data.

IF YOUR COMPANY has a lot of consumer transactions, you can use that data to refine your customers' experience.

"Big data" is the latest buzz phrase. Cheaper computer storage and faster processing times let you analyze vast amounts of data more efficiently and more effectively than in the past.

Google has *enormous* data that it uses it a myriad of ways. It uses its GPS data to measure and improve traffic routes. From the data gained through search results, Google can make amazing predictions of where the next flu outbreak will occur. It uses millions of voice interactions in its creation of speech recognition software.

Netflix has vast amounts of data from its millions of subscribers. It uses the data to enhance its customers' experience with the Netflix services. For example,

from analysis of the movie preferences of customers, Netflix is able to predict other movies in its database that those customers will enjoy in the future.

Amazon does the same with its big data. It accumulates data on millions of customer purchases, and then uses it to recommend other products customers might enjoy. With big data, you can analyze customer transactions, complaints, large purchases, and more, to find patterns that will help you improve customer experience and increase sales.

Not just Internet-based companies use big data to fine-tune their customer experience. Weather Channel (The Weather Company), Coca Cola, UPS, and Big Lots are some of the businesses that make use of big data from their own experience as well as purchased data to refresh their value and experience.

There's a wealth of knowledge in that big data.

Solve a need and disrupt an industry.

PEOPLE NEED TO get places. Taxis can be costly, unpleasant, or unavailable. Enter Uber.

Uber has innovated the customer transportation experience. The company has disrupted the structure of the taxi service by putting customers in the role of transportation dispatcher using their smartphones. What makes Uber better and different? 1) Anywhere and anytime 2) Ride in style and 3) Leave the cash at home.

Uber has grown amazingly quickly. Started in 2009, its service in 2015 is available in over 55 countries and 250 cities around the world with an estimated $40 billion valuation. Uber has integrated the physical and digital experience, allowing customers to track their driver on a map with their mobile device until their ride arrives.

Uber has many energized advocates who rave about the service. The only consistent objections are from taxicab companies (they hate the competition) and from consumers about Uber's market demand pricing when prices can spike temporarily.

Uber has felt some bumps in the road. But it's a great example of how solving the customer's need can be the start of something really big.

Apologize with actions as well as words.

WE ALL LIKE it when a company apologizes after making a mistake. But we like a company much better when it backs its apology with action.

Take the airline industry. They've developed a "Sorry Science" to apologize for misdeeds. It's part of their customer loyalty programs. Apologies range from "We're sorry" e-mails, to selecting a fitting apology letter from a vast "sorry" library, to far-ranging frequent flier mileage awards. Dedicated agents, trained to be sincere, deliver apologies directly to customers over the phone and Internet.

While there is nothing wrong about apologizing for bad service, it is not enough. Airlines scored lower on Forrester Research's 2014 Customer Experience

Index than many retailers. This may be because consumers are frustrated by the airlines' slow response times or the fact that they are not really solving their problem.

Saying "I'm sorry" is a good start. But actually solving a customer's problem is better.

Measure what matters to your customers.

WHEN FOCUSING ON customer experience, forget typical measurements such as customer acquisition and retention. These statistics mean much more to the company than to the customer and typically exclude insights about the emotional components of the customer experience.

Look at factors relevant to your customers. According to Joely Gardner, CEO of Human Factors Research, measure customer experiences such as: How long did it take for a customer to receive a package? How many layers are in your automated phone tree before your customer can talk with a real person?

To determine what matters most to customers, conduct focus groups and in-depth interviews. Listen to your customers and you'll learn what you're doing right and, more importantly, how you can improve your process.

Examine other data, too, such as a review of help desk records (particularly complaints), social media commentary, and discussions with salespeople.

Gardner recommends having a combination of qualitative information and quantitative data. "I love numbers, numbers are great. But numbers never tell you why. You absolutely have to have the interviews to understand why people give an experience a high or low rating."

The more you understand what matters to your customers' interactions with your business, the more opportunities you will find to make the customer experience better.

Start selling before the sale.

PAY ATTENTION TO the pre-transaction experience.

"Consumers are changing the way they choose their cars," says Chrissy Totty, head of innovation at BMW's media planning agency, Vizeum. "It is a very different experience from even five years ago."

Now, instead of visiting dealers, collecting brochures, and listening to sales pitches, 70 percent of all people in the market for a car start by spending time online gathering information about models, options, and prices. They read websites, professional and amateur auto reviews, and tap their social networks before they buy. Some buy online, and others go to a dealer having decided on the exact specifications of their purchase.

Similar changes are taking place in other markets. The Corporate Executive Board (CEB) surveyed more than 1,400 B2B customers across multiple industries, and found that 57 percent of a typical purchase decision is made before a customer talks to a supplier.

You need to start engaging your customers and selling before customers enter your business. If you ignore the pre-transaction experience, you are very likely sending those prospects to your competitors.

Create personas.

IT'S AS IMPORTANT to know your customers beyond demographics of income, geography, age, gender, and psychographics of lifestyles or business. Successful companies create "personas" of their typical customers, by trying to understand what makes their customers tick as well as seeing them as just statistics.

A persona is a fictional customer who represents a real segment of your audience.

Here's how to create a persona:

- use a photo of a "typical" customer

- include a quote that captures the persona's main concern, challenges or objective

- describe a day in the life of the persona

- describe how the persona uses the Internet, including pre-purchase use

- discuss what devices the persona prefers

- develop a story about which social media the persona chooses, how it is used, and how it influences the persona

- describe the persona's buying process

- consider what the persona would like your customer experience to do for him/her

Bring your persona to life! Mitchell International, a tech company that handles property and casualty claims, creates personas for their B2B insurance clients. The personas are available on their company Internet, and they also have life-sized cardboard versions of personas throughout their offices. The personas are updated regularly by spending time with the kind of people the personas describe.

Great personas lead to great customer experience for real people.

Design for people.

HUMAN-CENTERED DESIGN is a simple and effective way to create a virtuous feedback loop for the total customer experience.

Design a product or service with input from people who are likely to use it. At every stage of development, from prototype to market, have real people test it. Refine the product or service with their feedback until actual users report that it is as good and easy to use as it can be.

This is not a new concept. Kellogg used a version of human-centered design to develop and refine corn flakes in the late 1800s. Modern companies such as Warby Parker and Etsy have embraced human-centered design to improve their products and services.

Human-centered design works for improving the overall customer experience, including your people, messages, processes, and services. Test your development with real people who closely match your present and future customers to improve your company's total customer experience.

Keep people in the loop while you develop a complete experience.

Make sure your products and services work in the real world.

MANY PRODUCTS OR services that look great on paper fail when real customers try to use them in real time. The great customer experience companies watch customers actually using their products or services in real-life situations in order to refine their offerings.

For instance, the now-ubiquitous Apple retail stores started as one prototype store near Apple's headquarters. At this prototype store, Apple tested various ways to provide customer service, display products, and offer advice via the "Genius Bar." After testing their products and services in real situations in the prototype store, Apple was able to confidently roll out their successful Apple stores.

Netflix uses an in-house customer experience lab to do A/B testing. Netflix employees watch real

people in the lab who are watching shows and movies through the Netflix system, then use the information to make customer experience improvements.

Customer experience labs are not just for large companies with big budgets. A makeshift lab is perfect for a small business. You can do this within your retail environment, or use a conference room and bring in customers to observe. The key is to make your "lab" as close to the actual customer environment as possible. You must have a procedure to observe and compare different ways of presenting products and services.

Test. Learn. Revise. Then roll out.

Test the out-of-box experience.

A HIGH RETURN rate causes a significant blow to a company's bottom line. In some industries, that return rate is so high that profits are hard to come by. Retail consulting firm Kurt Salmon reported in May 2013 that online consumers return 20 to 30 percent of apparel and soft goods. Often the problem comes just as the customer is taking the product out of the box.

I conducted out-of-box testing for a consumer electronics company that was having millions of dollars of returns of perfectly functional product. We created several internal teams made up of product managers, packaging engineers, salespeople, marketers, and engineers. Each team opened boxes of the company's products to examine the experience when the product arrived in the customer's home.

Some of the teams were surprised that assembly was required because there was no hint of this in any of the accompanying materials. One team smelled an odor like burnt toast when the product was turned on. Their response, like many purchasers, was to immediately unplug the device and return it. The engineers knew this odor was normal, but that fact was not mentioned in any of the information about the product. Testing the out-of-box experience was crucial: after improving the instructions to consumers, returns of the product were significantly lower.

Clothing and soft goods retailers, such as Nordstrom and Macy's, are working with Internet analytics companies Fashion Metric and True Fit to help customers determine more accurately how their online purchases will actually fit when they try them on at home.

Creating an out-of-box experience for customers that answers all their questions with no surprises will decrease your return rate and increase your bottom line.

Plan your customer's journey.

A CUSTOMER JOURNEY map can use text, photos, flow charts, and other illustrations and data to help show the many ways a typical customer interacts with your company. It can include touch points for people before a transaction, while a customer, and also when a customer acts as an advocate for the company. If your customers are not completing the journey in a way that maximizes sales and is pleasing to them, you have to consider changing the interaction points where customers are getting lost.

Here are five essentials for creating customer journey maps to improve your customer experience:

1   Agree on when a customer experience begins with your company. Usually, it starts *before* a

prospect becomes a customer.

2   Determine the most important ways a customer can interact with your company before, during, and after a transaction.

3   Decide on the use of the map. The map can be used to understand the current customer experience or it can help determine a new customer experience.

4   Keep your customer journey map updated.

5   Include measures of emotion, economics, and time impact on the customer.

If you know where your customers are going, you can help make their journeys more pleasant and rewarding both for the customer and for your bottom line.

Be a fly on the wall.

WHAT IF YOU could be part of a group of people and, without influencing them, learn about what they want and what they need? In the world of cultural anthropology this is known as "ethnographic field research." I call it "blending in." Whatever it's called, it is a useful method for understanding people's behavior in the actual locations where they use products or services.

Ford used ethnographic field research in the late 1990s to revive the new Mustang. Consultants rode along with people in their Mustangs, watching them and interviewing them while they drove. They wanted to know what customers meant when they said they wanted the feeling of "power" while driving. Ford used those findings to redesign the Mustang to make it "look fast."

At Intuit, they use a process called "Follow Me" to observe people engaging with their products and services in their offices and homes. Co-founder Scott Cook initiated the practice early in Intuit's history. He understood that watching people use the company's products in the actual places where they work or live gives invaluable insights into how the software, manuals, or support can be improved. Intuit employees observe customers' behavior: the notes people make to themselves to help them use a product or get support, the frustrations customers have when accessing and using a product for the first time. The company then uses those findings for product, service, and support improvement.

Blend in and observe customers to learn valuable insights about how your product or services are used in the real world.

Begin a great customer experience with a pleasing user experience.

TRYING SOMETHING NEW for the first time can be challenging, time-consuming, and cause anxiety. One way to encourage people to try a new product or service is to develop a positive user experience, according to Tom Parham, principal of Technology Leadership Services.

Part of the secret is to blend in some familiarity. Begin with something customers have already used successfully and enjoy. You'll have to test the new product or service with people who are likely users, and then refine and test again. When you enter the market with your new product or service that has had the "bugs" removed, your pleasing user experience will be the start of an overall great customer experience.

Parham says, "User experience is a change manager that helps people do things that are not visible to them now. It inspires you to go there. To leave behind what just became old for the new ways."

When you start with a great user experience, great CX is likely to follow.

Blend digital and physical.

HOW SUCCESSFULLY YOU blend your digital and physical customer experiences can make or break your business. If people are comfortable with the digital presence you offer, they tend to include it as a seamless and spontaneous part of their lives.

Start by understanding how and when customers access your website or mobile app and under what conditions they do so (will they be in a rush, on a noisy subway, or sitting at their desks?). Then consider their visit to your physical location.

Starwood Hotels and Resorts Worldwide is moving to blend its digital and physical customer experiences with a personalized app for guests of its Westin chain. Two days before guests arrive at the hotel, they receive photos of attractions and information about local shopping. The address of the hotel is shown in the local language(s) to make it easier for a guest going from airport to the hotel. The app is at the heart of a larger strategy to drive customer loyalty. Guests can decide to register in person at the front desk or digitally on their smartphones.

Create smooth transitions between the digital and brick-and-mortar customer experiences for your company.

Make your product easy to use.

LOOK AT THE top of your closet or the back of a desk drawer. You'll find something—a product, a piece of software—that is just gathering dust, pushed aside in frustration because the item was harder to use than *not* to use.

Harry Hersh, co-author of *The Human Factor: Designing Computer Systems for People*, says, "Using any tool should be easier than not using those tools. In woodworking, for example, hand tools are often more efficient than power tools."

Hersh says that video games are examples of how a product can compel usage. He says that a user starts playing a video game and immediately becomes entranced.

Scott Cook and Tom Proulx founded Intuit on the basis that using a personal computer for accounting could be easier than traditional accounting with pencil and paper. Their first product, Quicken, lived up to this ideal.

If your product is not intuitive and immediately useful, change your product's design.

Develop online concierge services to deliver customer experience.

CONCIERGE SERVICES USED to be the province of the rich—someone who made your reservations at a high-end resort or ran errands at a luxury apartment building for the tenants. But on the Internet, concierge services are technologies that help shoppers use their time more productively.

The Bouqs Company, an online florist, offers a concierge service that sends flowers on a schedule that customers choose:

- Regular Blooms: Flower delivery at set, regular intervals.

- Never Forget: Calendars and reminders that send flowers on the important dates.

- Just Because: Random, surprise deliveries.

Customers of The Bouqs appreciate the experience of selecting the flower delivery schedule that works best for them and helps them look like a hero. It's quick, easy, and the flowers are discounted from their regular prices.

Consider how you can offer concierge services online that will improve your customers' experience with your company.

Segment customers by experience.

THE HOLY GRAIL of customer experience is one that has been purposefully built by a company. The company considers: What should the customer experience be? and then consciously creates a complete experience to answer that question.

But one size (or one experience) doesn't fit all. Segments or groups of customers may require different experiences. If your company can tailor the customer experience to a variety of customer segments, it will be on track to providing every customer with a great experience.

Four Seasons Resorts knows that its customers have many different preferences for a vacation. They offer a variety of hotel options based on the customer's interest in beaches, skiing, family travel, golf, and more. For each vacation option, Four Seasons provides different hotel choices, different activities, and a different customer experience. Everyone is happy.

Market segmentation used to be based on needs, economics, and demographics. But today's segmentation based on customer experience relates to what the customer wants to get from your product or service. For a supermarket, customer can be segmented this way: those who prefer home delivery, those who call in their order but pick it up at the store, and those who come in the store and select for themselves. Each segment will have a different customer experience with the store, which can be tailor-made for each segment.

Think about what your customers want from your products or services. Do they divide into a number of segments? Then create a customer experience designed especially for each.

View customer support as a product.

CUSTOMER SUPPORT PLAYS a big part in creating a great customer experience. One way to make sure your company emphasizes support is to think of support as part of the product.

This means developing your support experience as an integral part of the customer experience and making sure it contributes significantly to customers' needs. The customer experience you offer depends on that seamless product support that assures customers they made the best choice and helps you deliver on your promises.

The Genius Bars at the Apple Stores exemplify this idea. Apple has made support part of the retail store, not a side department that's hard to access. Apple customers can get the support over the phone

or webchat, too. Support for Apple products is part of the products, and it's that support that is largely responsible for creating customers who are advocates for the company.

BMW now has its own "Geniuses" who provide product support much the way it's done at Apple—in BMW dealerships, through a smartphone or tablet app, and by phone. The post-purchase experience includes an "encore" visit with a BMW Genius, one-on-one, to insure that the new BMW owner is comfortable with all the features and functions of the new car.

Support your local customer!

Design your products and services with customers in mind.

BUSINESSES ARE OBSESSED with solving problems in an analytical way. Define all the parameters of a problem and you're sure to come up with a product or service that consumers want.

"Design thinking" goes a little bit deeper. It gives companies the ability to imagine various paths to a product or service that elegantly solves a problem. Steps in design thinking include interviewing consumers or business people, developing personas (aka user profiles), and creating and testing prototypes of products, services or messages with people who match personas. Design thinking recognizes that there are many paths to solve a particular problem or see an opportunity and that the most straightforward solution may not be the best long-term solution.

You would expect companies like Google and Apple to use design thinking in their approaches to innovating new ideas—and they do (Google allows workers 20 percent of their time just "to think"). But other companies are also employing the concept of design thinking in their operations. Kaiser Permanente used design thinking to identify "22 key experiences" patients have when going through Kaiser's health care system. Then Kaiser worked to make those experiences better.

Sharon Carmichael, Senior Interaction Design Manager at Intuit, told me, "If a company wants to be at the top of its game for customer experience, design thinking experts need to be at the leadership table." Key business decisions will then be based on designs proven with the customer.

By using design thinking from strategy to operations, you are positioning your company for CX leadership in the long term.

Embrace new branding techniques.

APPLE, DISPLACING LONGTIME leader Coca-Cola, is now the most valuable global brand in the world. According to BrandZ, in a report issued in May 2015, Apple's brand value increased an amazing 67 percent in one year!

Branding is a twentieth-century concept, but companies are using new branding techniques to enhance twenty-first-century customer experience. For instance, New Balance launched a #SeeMyRun campaign in which they sent Fresh Foam shoes to "brand champions," who responded with video and images on runs with the new shoes.

Fine & Raw chocolate factory enables you to

drink a shake or delight in a chocolate treat while you enjoy the smells of chocolate products being made.

Kohler markets their toilets and faucets like works of art to attract high-end consumers.

Brand marketing is so crucial to customer decision making that cities are using sophisticated branding techniques to attract tourists. One of the most successful is "What Happens in Vegas, Stays in Vegas." That slogan gives potential visitors the sense of excitement and possibility with an undertone of naughtiness that sums up the attraction of Las Vegas.

By embracing your brand, you help potential customers immediately recognize what you Do-For them that they value.

Watch the clock!

WE ALL FEEL the pinch of limited time in our lives. Your product or service must be so compelling that customers will choose to spend time with it.

Netflix understands that its customers have plenty of other entertainment options at its fingertips besides Netflix. There is only so much time for entertainment and Netflix wants to fill that time with its offerings.

Netflix makes a compelling argument for customers' time by:

- **Using sophisticated software to recommend additional films and shows.** By suggesting other movies that their customers will enjoy,

Netflix helps consumers save time deciding what to watch.

- **Offering new and innovative programming.** Original programming created for Netflix alone, such as "House of Cards" and "Orange Is the New Black," give customers content that extends Netflix's share of their time allocated to entertainment.

- **Offering content via both streaming and traditional DVDs.** By giving customers choices and different price plans, Netflix allows customers the ability to select the service as they want to receive it.

Tempus fugit (time flies)! Your customer experience will help you get the largest share of your customer's time as they can give you.

RULE
32

Discover the "influencers."

MANY BUSINESSES FOCUS solely on their own messages and advertising, assuming that customers and potential customers will get their information directly from them. This assumption, which always had an element of wishful thinking, is less true today than ever.

Customers turn to independent sources of information known as *influencers*. These can include trusted experts, friends, and social media. Give your company an advantage by crafting an informative and valuable experience for the influencers of your customers.

The *Wall Street Journal* found that the key influencers of mutual fund customers are independent financial websites and publications, not the information provided by the fund companies themselves. Sixty-six percent of customers relied on those independent websites and other publications to make mutual fund decisions. Twenty-four percent checked a company's own website, and only ten percent used the official fund prospectus as their chief source of information.

Who are your customers' influencers? There may be some instances where influencing the influencers is more important that anything you can do directly.

Research how customers are making their buying decisions. If customers rely on information from select social media to choose your product, then you need to have a strong social media presence in the right places. If independent advisory websites and blogs influence your customers' buying decisions about your product or service, seek out those web sites and top bloggers and give them the information that shows the strengths of what you are offering.

Identifying, understanding, and reaching out to influencers can be just as important as trying to reach customers directly.

Fail your way to success.

FAILURE IS AN intrinsic part of the learning process.

In his 2014 *60 Minutes* interview, Elon Musk, CEO of Tesla Motors, said, "I didn't really think Tesla would be successful. I thought we would most likely fail. But I thought that we at least could address the false perception that people have that an electric car had to be ugly and slow and boring like a golf cart." Said Musk, "If something is important enough, you should try. Even if the probable outcome is failure."

At his rocket company SpaceX, the first three rockets failed to reach orbit. Where does Musk put the limit? "A fourth failure would have been absolutely game over." But flight four was faultless, rewarded

by NASA with a $1.5 billion contract to SpaceX.

Apple has become so phenomenally successful that people forget it has had its share of failures. The Lisa computer in 1983 was its first computer to include the mouse, but it failed miserably in the marketplace. That failure evolved into the phenomenal success of the Macintosh. Apple's palm-sized computer, the Newton MessagePad, bombed after its introduction in 1992. But the Newton paved the way for the dominance of the computer we all carry with us—the smartphone.

There is an energizing edginess about a company willing to tempt failure in a bold embrace of the future.

Create a great working environment.

IF YOUR EMPLOYEES love you, there is a good chance your customers will, too. There is a strong and growing connection between the best places to work and companies with the strongest customer experience commitment.

Nine of the companies in Fortune's 2015 list of the top 100 best places to work are businesses recognized by independent researchers and experts as delivering exemplary customer experiences. Three of these "experience maker companies" are in the top ten: Google at number one, Quicken Loans at five, and Intuit at eight. Other companies with strong customer experience credentials on the list include: Wegmans Food Markets, USAA Insurance, Kimpton Hotels & Restaurants, Zappos.com, Nordstrom, and Four Seasons Hotels.

What makes a company great to work for? Here's what goes into the metrics of the Best Places to Work Index:

- Management credibility

- Job satisfaction and camaraderie

- Strong pay and benefit programs

- Best hiring practices

- Clear-cut internal communication

- Employee training programs

- Employee recognition programs

- Diversity efforts

When you treat your employees right, your customers will also benefit.

Flatten your organizational structure.

BUSINESSES THAT ABANDON top-down vertical organization to develop horizontal teams and expertise create better customer experience. Flattening the organizational chart gives employees more responsibility and creates opportunities to communicate with peers across the company. But it also benefits customers with a more immediate and consistent experience.

At the Ritz-Carlton hotels and at Hampton Inns, employees are given wide berth to solve problems. Hampton Inn employees can offer refunds and even free nights to solve customer complaints without taking the problems to managers.

Companies that rely on managers to solve small tasks just cause customer confusion. A local drugstore requires a manager to approve any refund, no matter how small. Why would a company spend a manager and employee's salary and hold up a checkout line for ten minutes to give approval to a three-dollar return?

Think horizontally. Not vertically.

Reject customer satisfaction!

CUSTOMER SATISFACTION DOESN'T necessarily indicate great customer experience. Customer satisfaction is simply the difference between what a customer expects and what a customer gets. If expectations are low, then satisfaction can be high, even when the customer experience is poor.

Don't measure your customer experience by your satisfaction rates. Instead, look at whether you are creating advocates of your customers. Advocates not only buy every product or service you offer that they can use, they also actively encourage others to do the same. By offering a great customer experience, your end goal is to create advocates for your business.

Gary Tucker, CEO at DealerRater, says, "Exceptional customer experience can best be measured by behaviors like active advocacy and

loyalty. It is measured by what customers 'Say and Do.' Delighting customers across the entire experience can create active promotion, not only in the traditional social settings, but especially online... through social media and third party reviews."

Beware of setting the goal post too low. Go for delight, not satisfaction.

Create a customer experience center of excellence.

THIS CENTER DOESN'T need a lot of space. It can be maintained by one person at your company with input from all your staff. The center will gather and communicate the latest information about customer experience.

Here's what your customer experience center for excellence should contain:

- A library of books and resources. I recommend the following books: *The Experience Economy*, *Happy R.A.V.I.N.G. Customers!*, *The Customer Experience Revolution: How Companies Like Apple, Amazon, and Starbucks Have Changed Business Forever*, and *Don't Make Me Think*. Also, regularly consult the top customer and user experience websites such as: Uxpa.org, Jdpower.com, and Uxmatters.com.

- A library of interviews and presentations from people who work at companies known for their customer experience leadership and innovation. Many of these presentations are on YouTube with transcripts. Some video and audio interviews are exclusive and available only by rental through services like Netflix. There are some great talks by Steve Jobs, Jeff Bezos, and Howard Schultz available, for example. Other presentations may be found from independent research firms, user experience professionals, and valuation companies.

- Develop a list of the best customer experience companies both inside and outside your industry for reference. One place to start online is with the Temkin Experience Ratings, available at Temkinratings.com. Other CX indices also exist via paid subscriptions. Get familiar with the best CX companies to begin understanding what they do that you can use.

- Attend trade shows, conferences, and seminars about customer experience. Do this in small groups, from two to five people, including executives or owners, senior managers, and people who impact CX in your company. When you return, report what you learn and recommend changes.

- Participate in or start a customer experience special interest group (CXSIG) within your industry's association or as a stand-alone organization.

Your center will help your employees learn the newest and best techniques of developing a top customer experience company.

Be a proximity player.

WHEN ALL ELSE is equal, the shortest distance between the customer and the product or service can make all the difference. Proximity can be a game changer.

Back in the day when Blockbuster was a leader, renting a movie meant a trip to a retail store. In 1998, Netflix brought the movie to your mailbox—much closer to home. Now even the mailbox is too far—movies are streamed over the Internet directly into electronic devices in homes.

Apple Pay brought the proximity of the credit card transaction from the wallet to smartphone. Now, transactions are even closer—on your wrist with the Apple Watch.

So snuggle up and get close to your customers. It will pay off.

Recruit X-Men and X-Women.

THE X-MEN IN comic books and movies are super-heroes who fight for peace and equality. You need some X-Men and X-women, too—experts and innovators who can help your company stand out from the competition.

Google X is an advanced research lab. Their X-Men teams are made up of the best minds and people available. Google's CEO Larry Page calls them "Moonshots." Whether designing a driverless car, developing drone delivery, or creating contact lenses to monitor glucose levels for diabetic patients, these scientists are helping design a future with customers in mind.

I've had some experience with X-Men. While working at AT&T when the idea of managed data networks for businesses was very new, I was on a team that reviewed client proposals submitted by the data sales people and field network engineers. Our purpose was to determine which of these custom proposals might be the basis for a new market offer. Sometimes the level of complexity of a proposal required a fairly lengthy review period.

The sales people and network engineers sometimes asked in frustration, "Where's our answer? It's not rocket science, you know." What they did not know was that it was part rocket science. Many of the people I regularly sat next to on the review team were former rocket scientists from NASA.

You may not be able to hire former NASA rocket scientists, but you need your experimental experience people.

Get some X-Men and X-Women on board for innovation.

Don't fall in love with your great ideas.

INNOVATION IS NOT about ideas. It's about crossing the challenging idea-to-reality gap.

Steve Jobs dismissed the concept that innovative ideas are the key to success. Jobs said that people think "if you get a really great idea, it's 90 percent of the work. And if you just tell other people your great idea they can go off and make it happen."

He knew that wasn't true.

Jobs said, "Designing a product is keeping five thousand things in your brain, and fitting them all together. Every day you discover . . . a new problem or new opportunity to fit these things together a little differently. It's that process that is the magic."

Ideas may start the project, but the true genius is in the development.

If it ain't broke, fix it.

THE PERFECT TIME to invest in customer experience is when things are going well.

Summit Valuations is a residential and commercial real estate valuation company. When Ron Ahlensdorf Jr. became president in 2013, the company was producing great products and services.

But despite consistently positive customer feedback, Ahlensdorf saw that the company could be headed toward shrinking margins in the future due to increased competition in the valuation industry. He recognized that it was the right time to upgrade the customer experience.

Ahlensdorf's approach was to make Summit Valuations a solutions partner, not just a vendor of products. The company has improved its customer experience in a number of ways:

- High-touch, proactive, and dedicated customer service

- Attention to detail in every step of the valuation process

- Regular review meetings between Summit's quality assurance team and clients to continually adapt to changing market conditions

- Highly trained quality assurance specialists to review each client's specific reports based on their needs and qualifications

Don't wait until your company sees a downturn in profits before investing in customer experience. Do it when times are good to help strengthen those profits and customer relationships into the future.

Give a frictionless customer experience.

USING YOUR WEBSITE, interacting with an employee, and using your product should all be pleasing customer experiences. If everything goes well, the experience is "frictionless."

That's the goal, according to many customer experience leaders. But if the website says one thing and a customer rep says another, or the product doesn't work as promised, those interactions have painful friction points. Jack Dorsey, CEO of Square, says, "If you're not solving for the entire experience, you are putting those seams in front of the customers—and the customers see that. These friction points. . . actually slow down the business."

It's hard to give a frictionless customer experience, even when you control all of it. But when you don't control the entire experience, it can really be a challenge. Take the automobile industry, for example. Much of the customer experience of buying a car takes place at car dealerships, but auto manufacturers don't own the dealerships. Manufacturers are impacted by the customer experience delivered by the dealer, but can't control it. This is why customers are asked by manufacturers to complete surveys about their buying experience—and why the salespeople always ask the customers to rate them with a "10."

A positive customer experience with *every* company interaction is a hallmark of the best CX companies. To achieve that goal, you must make sure that all aspects of the customer experience, even those you don't totally control, are consistent and run smoothly.

Create positive feelings.

THE GREAT CUSTOMER experience companies understand that customers make purchasing decisions on more factors than a simple economic calculation. So those companies try to create positive feelings as well as dollars-and-cents value propositions.

Donald Norman, author of *Emotional Design: Why We Love (or Hate) Everyday Things*, is one of the leading authorities on emotion, design, and business. He explains that emotions drive value judgments, helping us decide whether something is good or bad, safe or dangerous. Even in a decision such as the purchase of fighter aircraft by the Air Force, there is a significant emotional component. Norman says, "You would be surprised how these cool, rational Air Force generals make decisions. They fall in love with the airplane. No matter what the facts say, they want that airplane. 'Twenty billion dollars? I don't care. This is the plane for me.' People who design these airplanes know that."

Positive results come from creating positive emotions.

Think like a shark.

IMAGINE YOU HAVE been selected to pitch your company on Shark Tank. You're going to be grilled by people trying to understand the core of your business.

You're entering the tank. The panel of venture capitalists has some questions for you to answer:

- Do you have a customer experience leader at your company?

- Do you have a social media connection with your customers?

- Do you test new ideas through research, customer usage, and use of prototypes?

- Do you keep all your promises to customers?

- Do you make sure all elements of the customer experience work to enhance your brand?

If you answer "yes" to all of these questions, you might get a shark to bite!

Make the experience genuine.

I HAVE BEEN going to the local branch of a large, 100-year-old national bank for many years. It's the closest one to me. The minute I walk in, whether there is a line of people or not, an employee greets me and tells me I'll be served very soon.

When I get to the teller window, the teller asks me how my day is going. The next questions I am asked are what can they do for me and would I like a bottle of water. After the transaction, under the watchful eye of a supervisor, the teller asks me if there is anything else he or she can do for me. Every time I go in there, the experience is exactly the same. Boring!

The bank is trying to enact a good system by laying down hard and fast rules for service— except . . .

The bank has not personalized the experience.

It's not genuine. It's the opposite of dealing with employees at a Four Seasons Hotel or an Apple retail store. In those companies, interaction is genuine. The employees get it. It's part of the company leadership culture and comes through the employees to the customers.

Customer experience that is genuine helps companies succeed. Canned interactions don't.

Define your business by
what it does for customers.

DEFINE YOUR BUSINESS not by its product, processes, or technology, but by what it does for customers.

Imprivata is an information technology company. Its main market is hospitals, but its business extends to banking, energy, and government. Imprivata provides authentication and access management, secure communications, and clinical workflow. These are their products and services. But you won't see a mention of that under the "What We Do" tab on the website. That's where you'll find what they do for *customers*: "Imprivata improves provider productivity for better focus on patient care," followed by details with some selected measures as examples.

Be clear about what you do for your customers. Imprivata is not defining itself by what it is making and selling today. That could change quickly based on numerous factors—regulations, new treatment discoveries—over which they have little control. But a need for improved productivity and focus on patient care is unlikely to ever go out of style.

Schwan's Home Service offers delivery of over 350 frozen products. Schwan's has an enviable online conversion rate that is consistently over forty percent year to year. This is how Schwan's describes its business and what it does for customers:

"Delicious food delivered right to your door: Order online anytime. 100% quality guarantee. Choices for everyone. No contracts or minimums."

Ask people in your company two questions:
- What business are we in?
- What do we do for customers?

Compare the answers. Ask customers what you do for them. Ask potential customers what you could do for them. Listen to the answers carefully and objectively. Boil them down to the essence.

That's the definition of your company.

Keep your customer experience lifecycle fresh.

SOMETIMES WHEN I am in front of an audience, I ask if there is anyone who still uses a BlackBerry. Rarely does a hand go up.

Only a few years ago, BlackBerry was the leading edge in smartphone technology. It seems like the BlackBerry experience became obsolete overnight.

BlackBerry's problems were caused by its competitors, Apple and Google (Android operating system). Apple redefined the market by incorporating a more up-to-date understanding of what customers wanted to do with their phones: use the Internet, listen to music, take photos. The development of apps, along with the finger touch interface, made the iPhone experience intuitive and effective. Google's Android

system created a similar experience for many smartphone brands.

BlackBerry didn't keep up with these changes that improved the smartphone's customer experience. Not even their customers loyal to the "real" keyboard could save the business. According to Gartner Research, BlackBerry's global smartphone market share in 2015 is 0.4 percent.

Leaders in customer experience compete with themselves to offer a more significant and valuable customer experience. If they don't keep improving their customer experience, someone else will.

Create a customer experience advisory board.

A BOARD OF directors advises the company about its overall business strategy. A customer experience advisory board is similar, but is specific to the topic of customer experience. If your company is serious about improving its customer experience, a key step is to create an advisory board dedicated to that end.

The job of a customer experience advisory board is to identify where the existing customer experience can be improved and to recommend when a new customer experience should be created. At least half of its members should be customer experience experts from outside the company.

The board should be no larger than a two-pizza team (see Rule 11). It should include customers and, if possible, non-customers who are similar to the new customers you want to have. But remember, this is not a focus group. It's a board developed to advise, so choose members carefully.

A customer experience advisory board can help you decide how, why, and when to change your customer experience.

Keep your promises.

IF YOU CAN'T deliver what you promise to your customers, your customers won't trust or respect you. More customers will complain about your faults than will praise your good deeds. And any exposed faults will have an exponential effect on other customers in social media.

If you promise that you will deliver books in two days (as Amazon does), you have to meet that promise. Books delivered in four days will lead to disappointment and complaints.

According to Janice Sutton, CEO and Executive

Editor of *Fleet Management Weekly*, "If you want to deliver a great customer experience, keep your agreements. They might be appointments, delivering a product, or providing a service. Don't assume customers will understand if you can't keep your promises."

Rate your company: what percentage of your promises do *you* keep?

Know social media.

SOCIAL MEDIA IS today's "word of mouth."

In the past, people made shopping decisions based on trusted friends' recommendations. Now, those recommendations have gone digital, encompass more people, and are crucial for the success of most businesses.

But social media options keep evolving. How are customers exchanging information about companies like yours? Yesterday it might have been TripAdvisor and Yelp. Today it might be Snapchat and Instagram. And tomorrow's hot button might not even exist yet.

Learn why your customers use social media, which social media they frequent, and what devices they use. How are they influenced? Do they become influencers by rating or writing?

J. D. Power's research shows that one-third of social media users get recommendations about a product or service from friends and family exclusively through social media. Today the most frequently used social media channels are Facebook (29 percent), followed by YouTube (19 percent) and Twitter (11 percent).

Social media is a major factor in business-to-business purchase decisions, too. Independent research firm International Data Corporation found that 75 percent of buyers worldwide use social media to support their purchase decisions.

Looks like we're all social animals.

Wall Street rewards the best customer experience.

HAVE YOU BEEN thinking, "This CX stuff sounds good, but it's ROI that really matters"?

Well, it turns out that the companies that lead in customer experience are also ones with highest return on investment.

According to Watermark Consulting's Customer Experience ROI Index, leaders in customer experience outperform the S&P 500 Index, while customer experience laggards trail far behind.

The 2015 CX ROI Index follows the top ten leaders and bottom ten laggards of publicly traded companies in Forrester Research's Customer Experience Ratings.

The index shows that customer experience leader companies generated a return 35 points higher than the S&P 500, and laggard companies 45 points lower than the S&P 500.

Watermark has been doing this analysis since 2007, and these results are consistent since that year. To quote the study: "It is, quite simply, a striking reminder of how a great customer experience is rewarded over the long-term, by customers and investors alike."

Customer experience is good for the bottom line.

Make magic happen!

GREAT CUSTOMER EXPERIENCE, when done really well, can feel a bit like magic. Consider what's being done today at Disney.

At Disney World, the theme park customer experience is being transformed by Magic Bands. The Magic Band eliminates tickets, allows the guest to enter the park, make dinner reservations, open their hotel room doors, get Fast Pass reservations to rides, and charge any purchases at the park.

With Magic Bands, Disney has raised the bar for responsive customer experience creation by tailoring the theme park experience to the needs of each guest. In the future, the Magic Band's RFID sensors will set off customized entertainment for the Band wearer. Characters will know Magic Band visitors by name, further personalizing the experience at the park.

Magic Bands also allow the park to know where every guest is at every moment. They can send characters to parts of the park and start parades to shift and move the guests around the park to better distribute the amount of people at any time of the day, further improving park efficiency and guest experience.

It's estimated that Disney invested about a billion dollars developing the Magic Bands. This is the kind of intensive design and development that insures an extraordinary customer experience and should bring Disney a significant long-term return on investment.

And it will, no doubt, set the bar for all theme parks in the future. Once you've experienced Disney World with the Magic Band, you'll expect the same frictionless customer experience at all the Disney parks, and at Universal, too.

After all, it's magic, isn't it?

Don't get distracted by the present.

THE TRULY GREAT customer experience leaders understand the past, see the present, and envision the future.

Leon Leonwood (L. L.) Bean was one of the early pioneers of customer experience. He recognized the value of customer service as more than an after-purchase fix. By personally testing the products he sold, he created a worry-free customer experience. Before other retailers, L. L. Bean allowed customers to experience the brand first through a catalog, and then through the flagship store. Beginning in 1951, the store was open 24 hours a day, 365 days a year. From the first time a customer looked at his catalog, to when they used the products and shopped in the store, L. L. Bean created a groundbreaking example of developing a seamless customer experience.

About twenty years ago, Amazon's Jeff Bezos looked into the future and created a customer experience that wasn't on anyone's radar screen. From the concept of being "the world's largest store" to creating the e-book category with the Kindle, to its innovative use of data to recommend products for customers, Bezos has built a company that continually is seen as one of the greats of CX.

When Larry Page and Sergey Brin founded

Google in 1997, their mission was to organize the infinite amount of information available on the Internet. Since then, Google has refined the customer experience of searching the Internet with ease of use and high quality results. Google dominated the field of Internet advertising with AdWords, set a new standard for mapping with Google Maps, and became the e-mail provider for hundreds of millions of users with Gmail. Google's Chrome redefined ease of browser use when it was introduced in 2008. Google continued to innovate with the introduction of Android, an open platform operating system for mobile devices. Android opened the door for developers of applications and services and for multiple brands of smartphones and tablets. Now Google works on perfecting technology for cars that can drive themselves. The Do-Fors include helping to prevent traffic accidents, freeing up people's time, and reducing carbon emissions. Thoughtful and purposeful customer experience has been at the center of all of Google's successful innovations.

Great customer experience leaders see the future, and it is theirs!

YOU GOTTA KNOW THE
Rules!

Also by Jeofrey Bean

In their innovative book, *The Customer Experience Revolution: How Companies like Apple, Amazon, and Starbucks Have Changed Business Forever*, authors Jeofrey Bean and Sean Van Tyne uncover valuable insights about leadership and decision-making. At large and small companies they call "Experience Makers," the focus has surpassed products, services, and price toward the purpose-built customer experience and the user experience within it.

$19.95
ISBN: 978-0-9826644-6-9
142 pp.

Available at
www.brigantinemedia.com

Made in the USA
Las Vegas, NV
10 November 2021